THE MUSIC TREE

TIME TO BEGIN
ACTIVITIES
English Edition

by
Steve Betts
with
Louise Goss
Sam Holland

English Version by Nadia Lasserson

Educational Consultants:

Steve Betts	Yat Yee Chong
Linda Christensen	Ted Cooper
Amy Glennon	Monica Hochstedler
Peter Jutras	Elvina Pearce
Mary Frances Reyburn	Craig Sale

Copyright © 2000 Summy-Birchard Music
a division of Summy-Birchard Inc.
This edition © 2000
All rights reserved   Produced in U.S.A.

Summy-Birchard Inc.
exclusively distributed by
Alfred Music
alfred.com

ISBN 1-58951-011-9

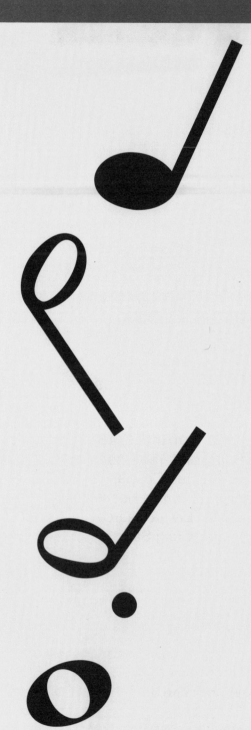

TO THE STUDENT:

You are starting an exciting adventure!
You'll be learning to play the piano, but even more important, you'll be learning all about music.

You'll learn how to **listen** to music, how to **read** it, how to **play** music at the piano and how to **compose** your own pieces.

To help you enjoy this new adventure, you'll have two companions:

 CHIP, a little chipmunk with great big eyes, who helps you see everything in the music.

 BOBO, a dog with long ears, who helps you listen to every sound you make at the piano.

Chip and Bobo will be with you at your lessons, but their main job is to help you practice. They'll remind you of the things you learned at your lesson, and what to do when you practice at home. With their help, we know you'll have a wonderful time learning to make music at the piano.

Draw lines matching the finger to the correct number.

Then colour the fingers:

Blue for 1   **Green for 3**   Red for 5

Orange for 2   **Purple for 4**

The first one is done to show you how.

5 4 3 2 1   1 2 3 4 5

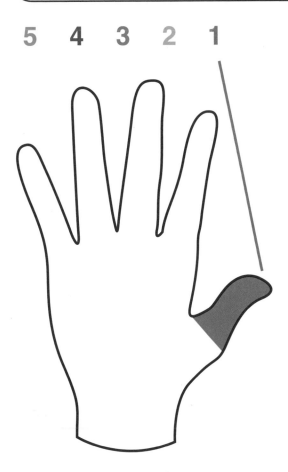
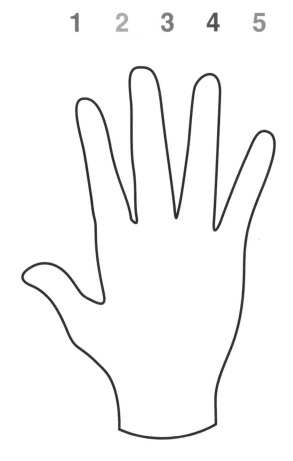

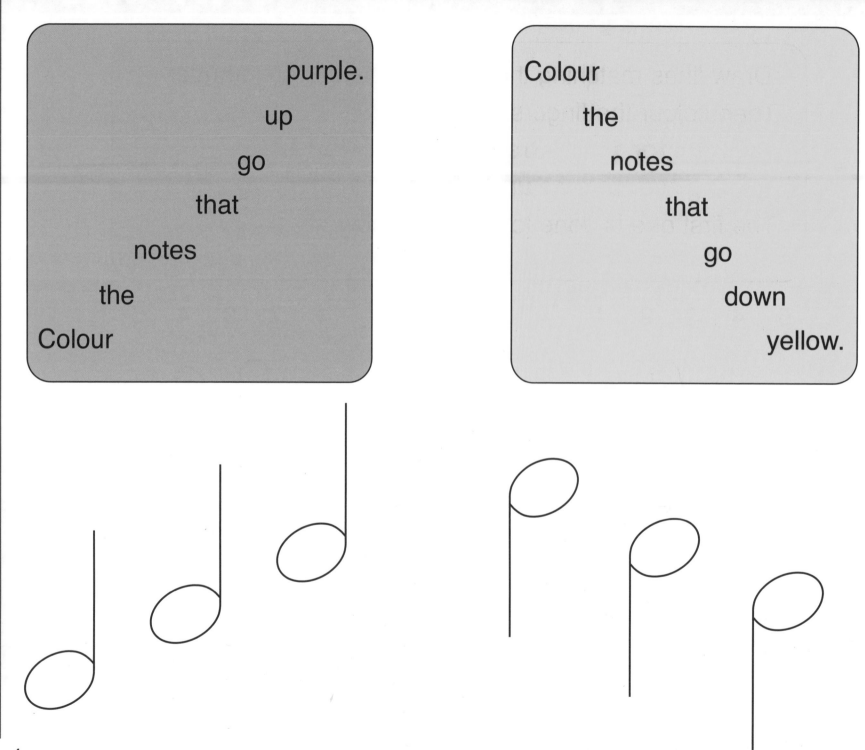

Colour the notes that go up purple.

Colour the notes that go down yellow.

4

Write the music alphabet going up.

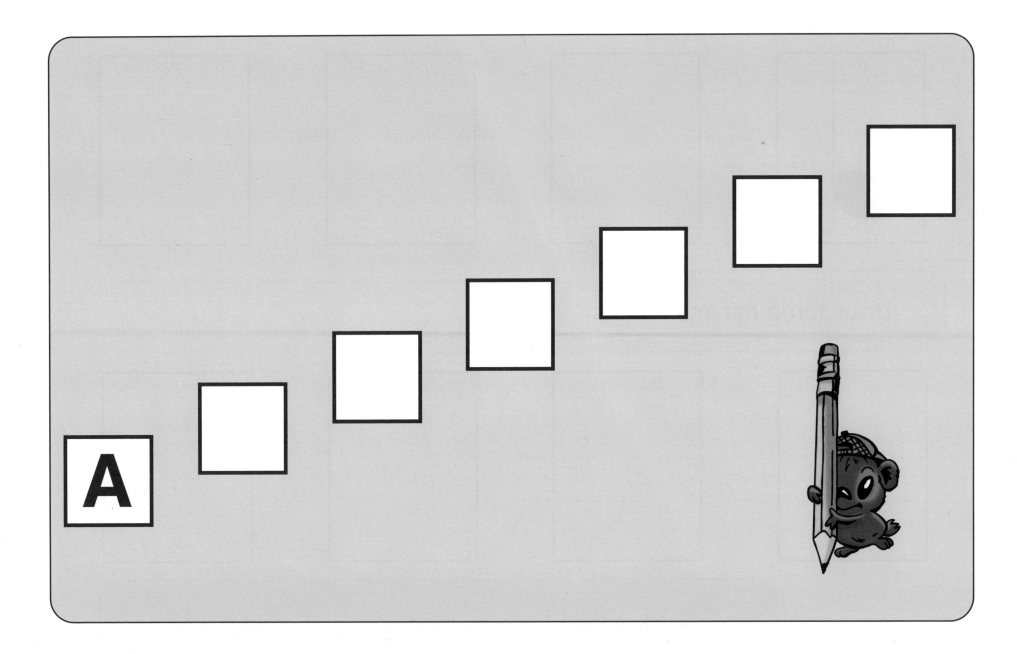

Draw three crotchets.

Draw three minims.

Each minim lasts as long as _____ crotchets.

Colour the keys:

Red for C

Yellow for D

Blue for E

Write the music alphabet going up and going down.

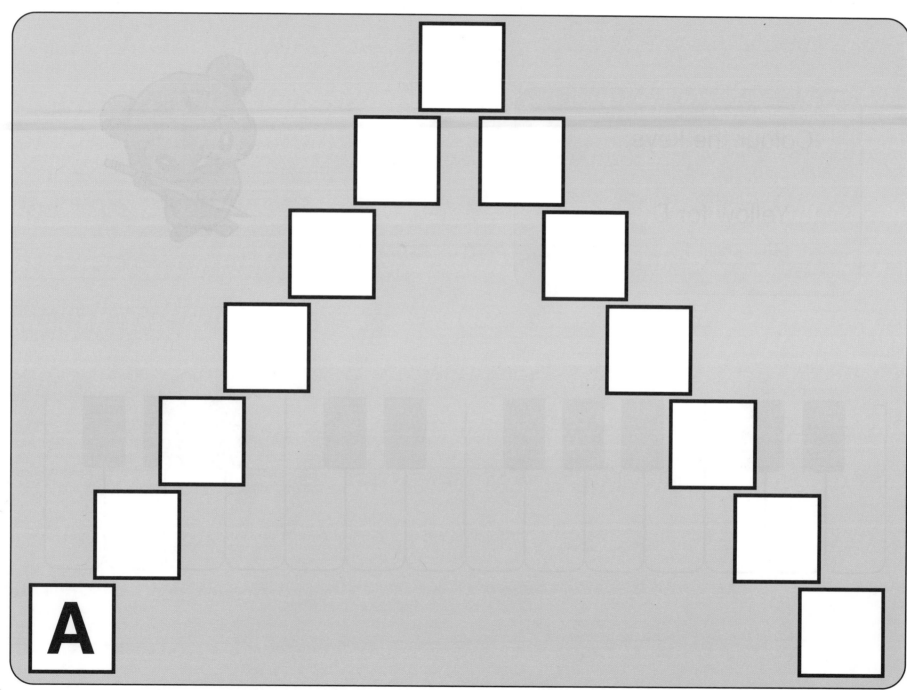

Match each sign to its name.
The first one is done to show you how.

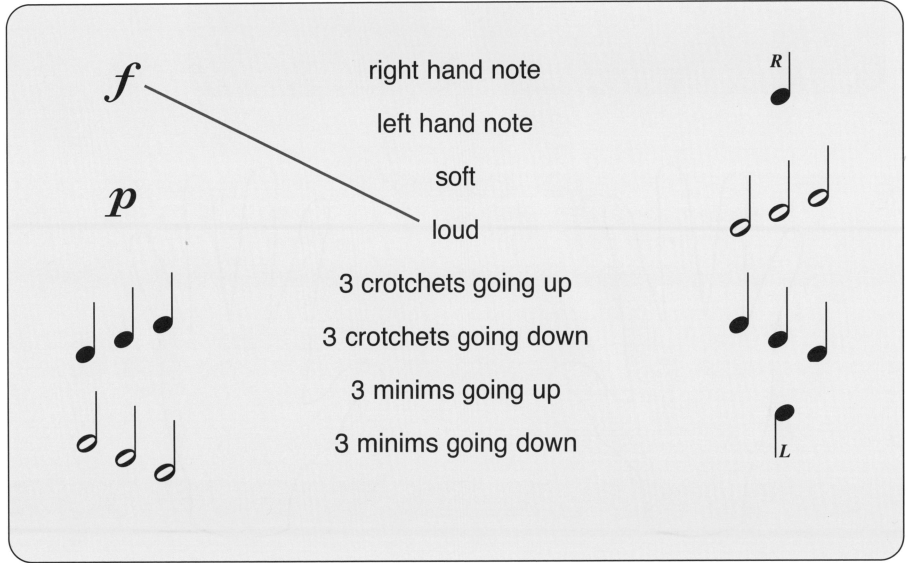

right hand note

left hand note

soft

loud

3 crotchets going up

3 crotchets going down

3 minims going up

3 minims going down

9

Colour the fingers:

Orange for 1　　　Red for 3　　　Green for 5

Purple for 2　　　**Blue for 4**

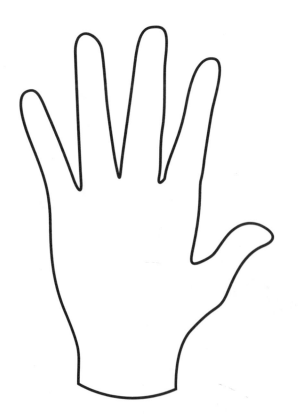 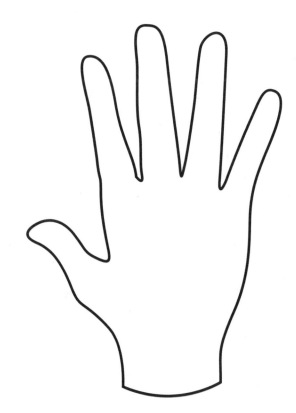

Colour
  the
    notes
      that
        go
          down
            purple.

                    yellow.
                  up
                go
              that
            notes
          the
Colour

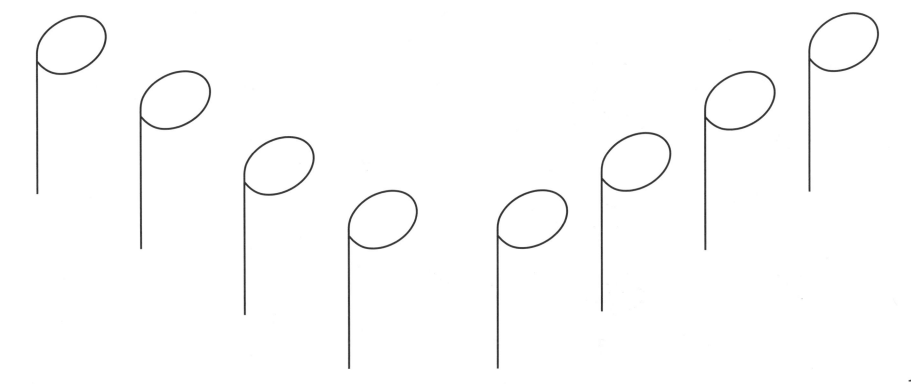

Colour the kites with crotchets orange.

Colour the kites with minims red.

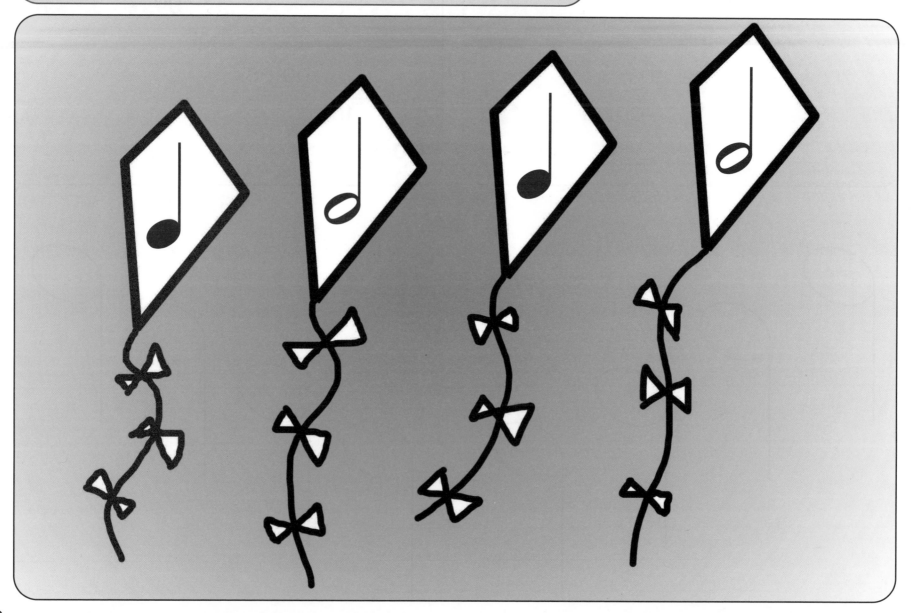

Colour the keys:

Green for A	Purple for D	Orange for F
Yellow for B	Blue for E	Brown for G
Red for C		

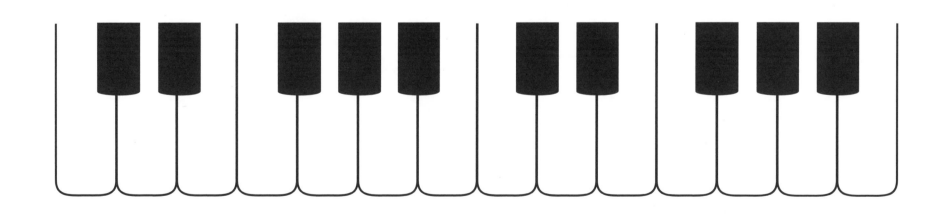

Write the music alphabet going up.

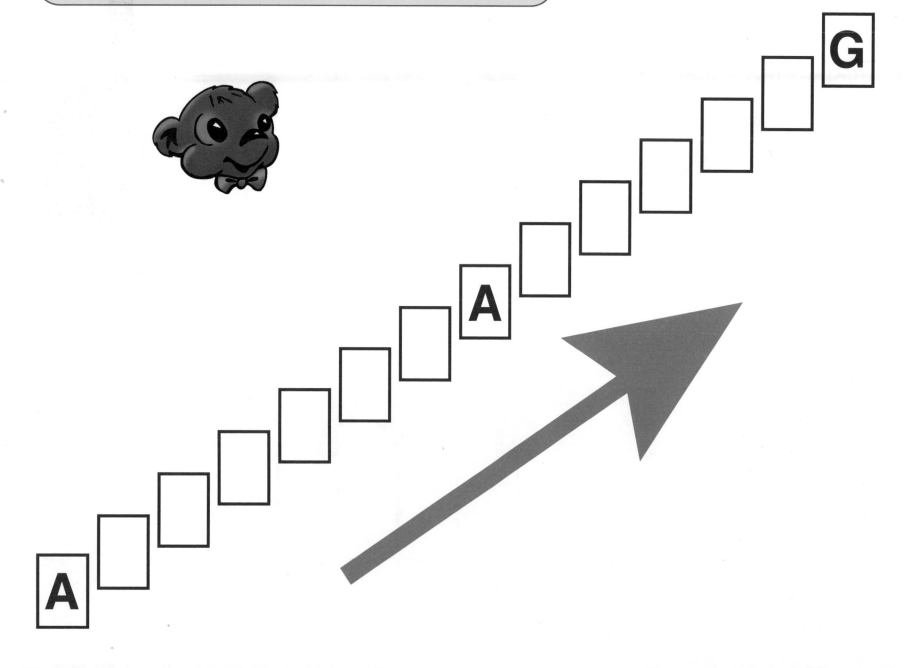

Write the music alphabet going down.

G

A

A

15

Colour the balloons:

Blue for notes going up

Yellow for notes going down

Red for repeated notes

Match each sign to its name:

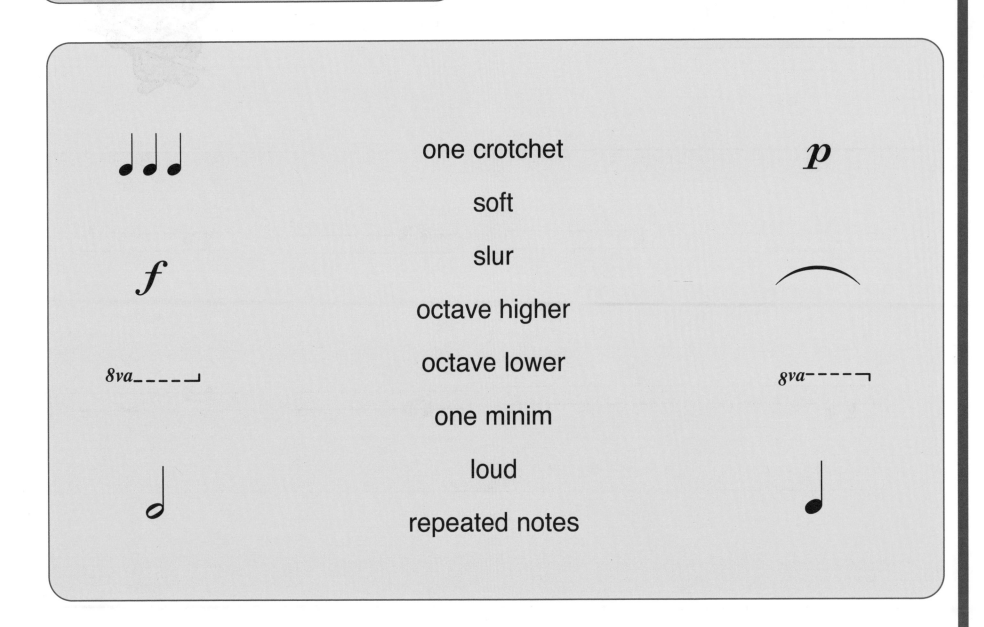

one crotchet

soft

slur

octave higher

octave lower

one minim

loud

repeated notes

Draw these seconds.

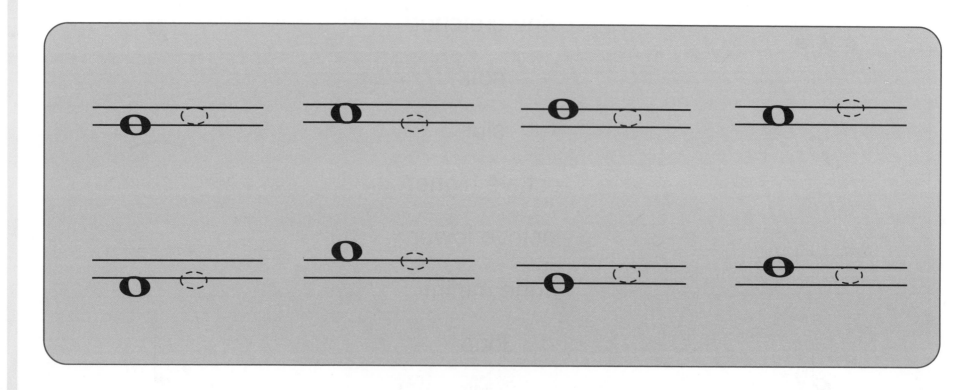

Music Math

Add or subtract the notes in each problem.
The first one is done to show you how.

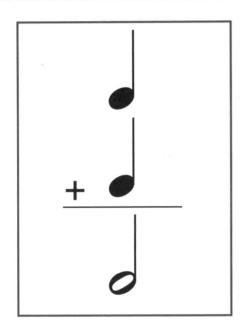

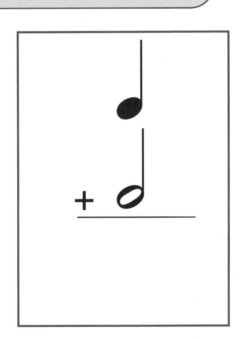

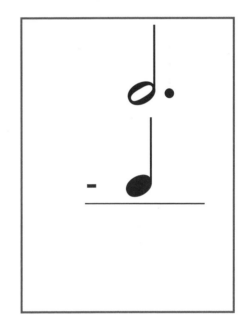

♩ + ♩ + ♩ =

19

Draw an **X** through the box that does not match.
The first one is done to show you how.

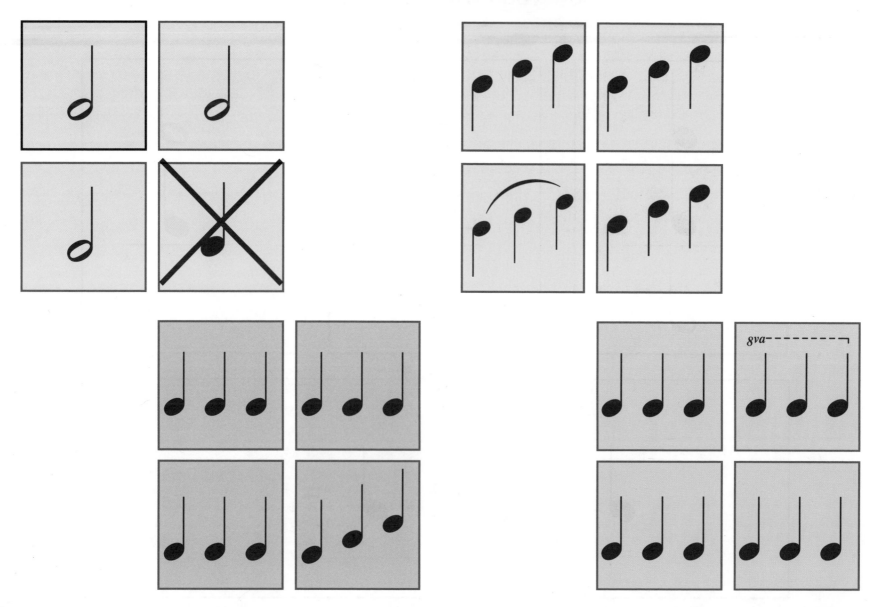

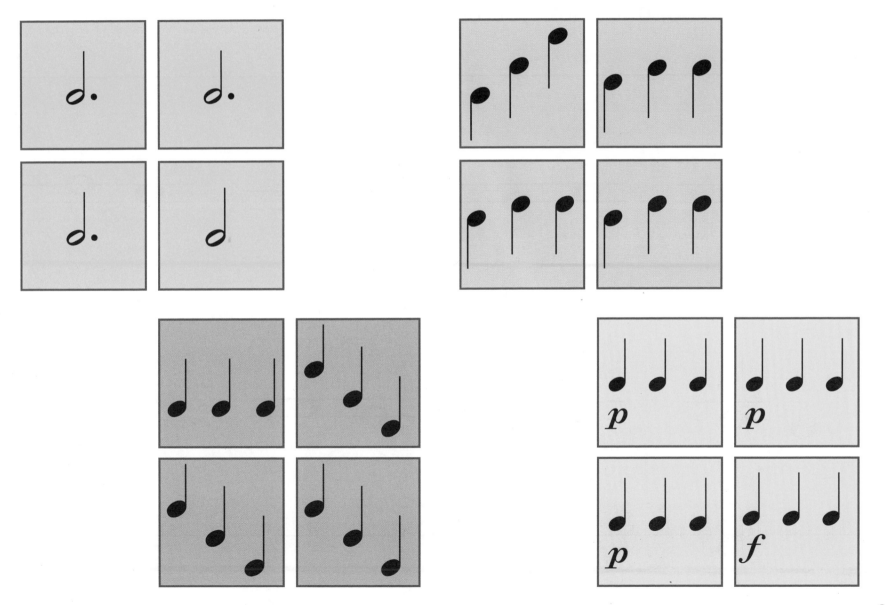

Draw an arrow up or down for each second.
The first one is done to show you how.

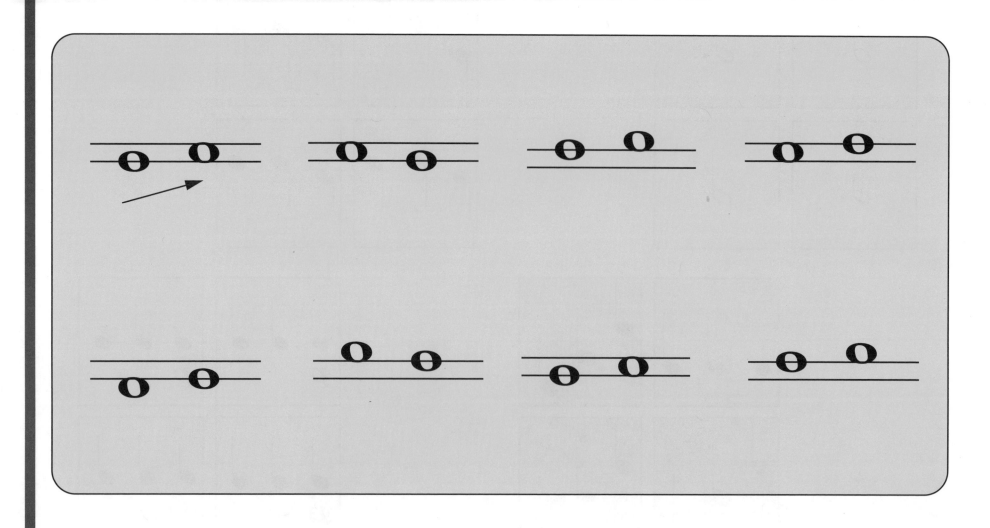

Draw an **X** through the box that does not match.

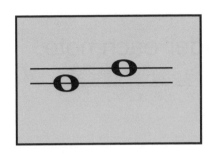 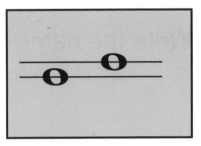

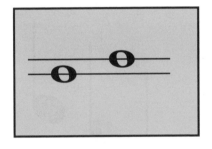 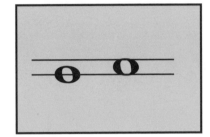

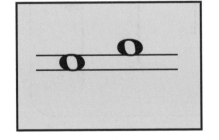 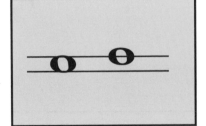

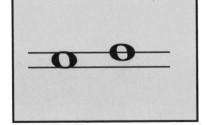 

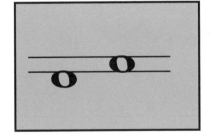 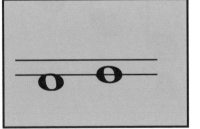

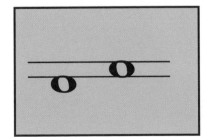 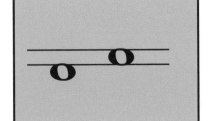

Write the name under each note.

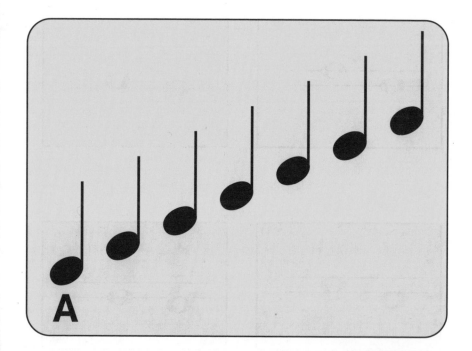

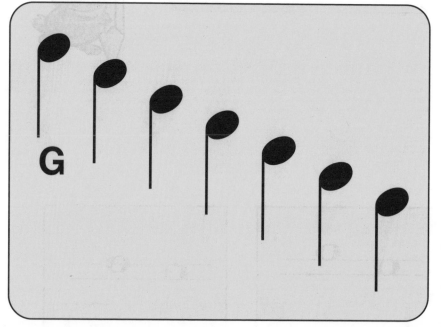

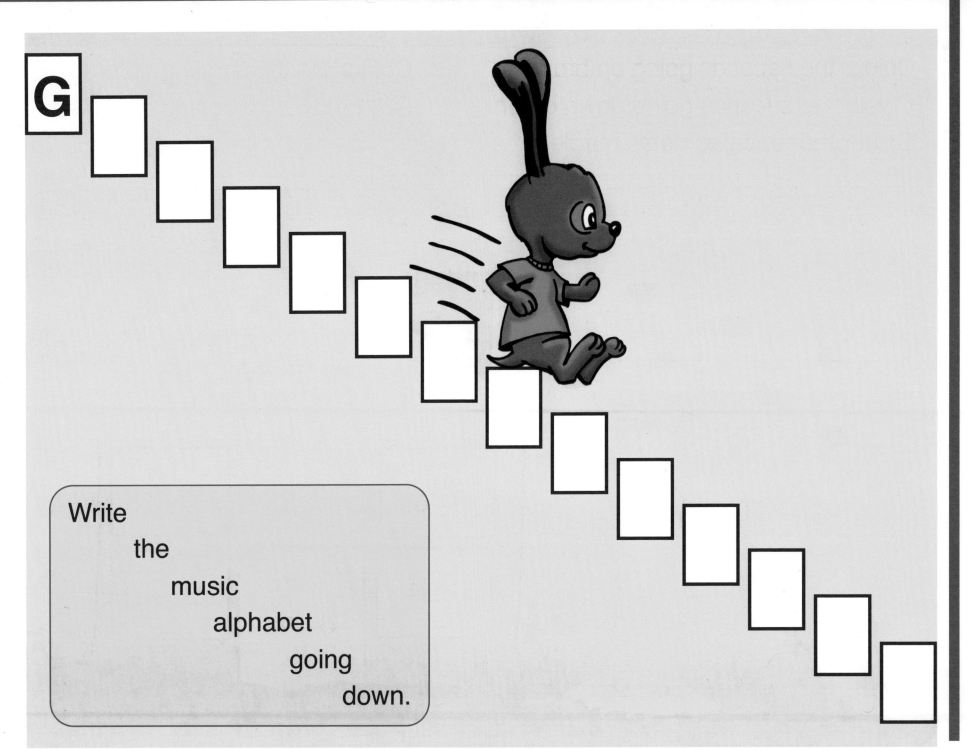

Write the music alphabet going down.

Colour the seconds going up brown.
Colour the seconds going down green.
Colour the repeated notes purple.

Colour the thirds going up orange.
Colour the thirds going down red.

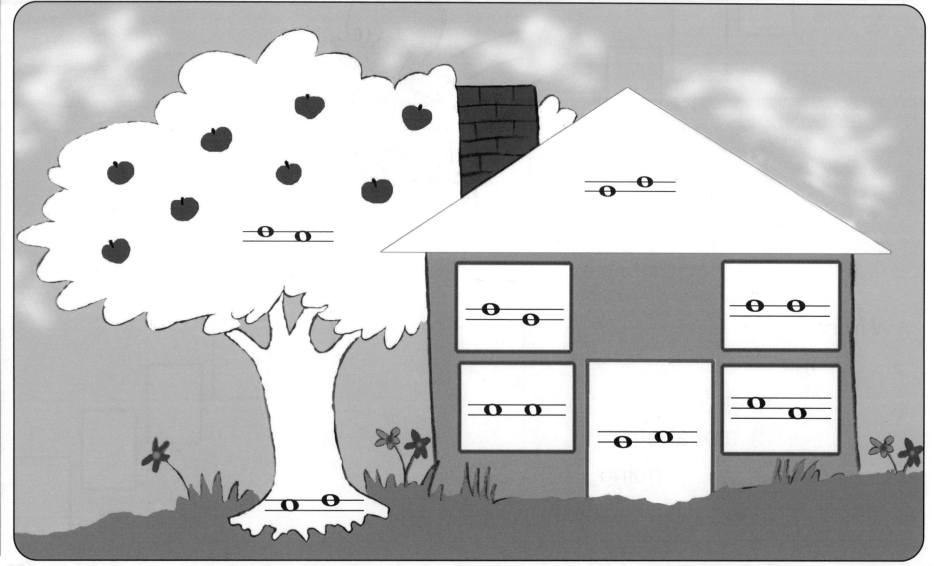

26

Draw a second above each note.

Draw a second below each note.

Help Chip find Bobo by following all the thirds!

Chip

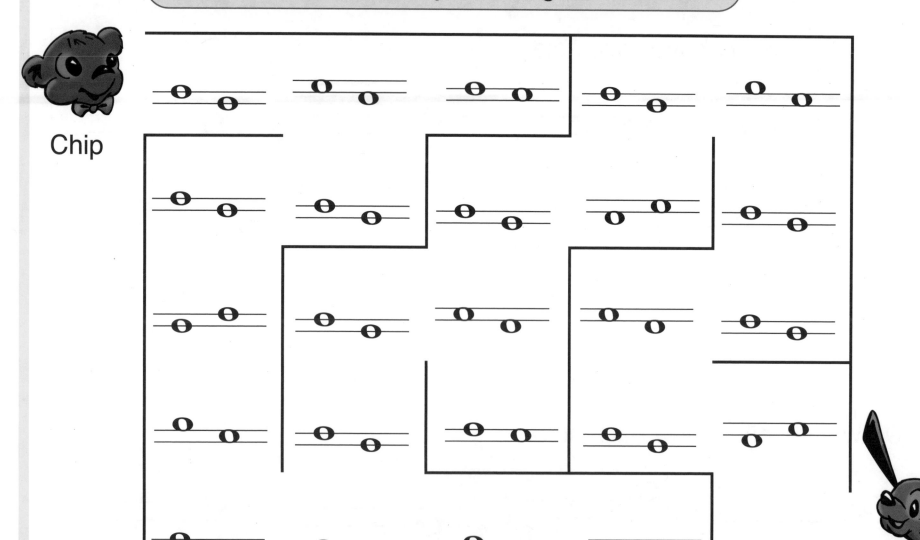

Bobo

Write the time signature for each rhythmic example.

Choose from   **2**   **3**   **4**   **5**

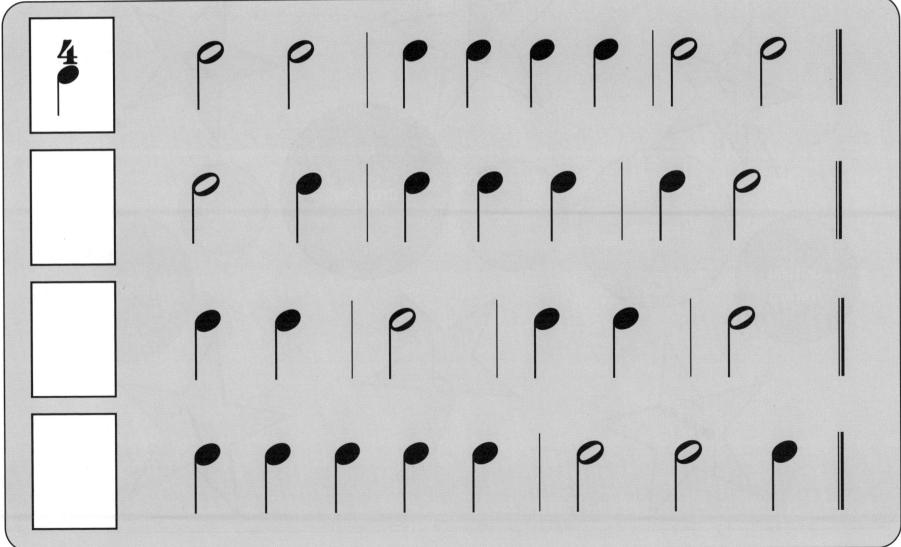

Match each star to the correct planet.
The first one is done to show you how.

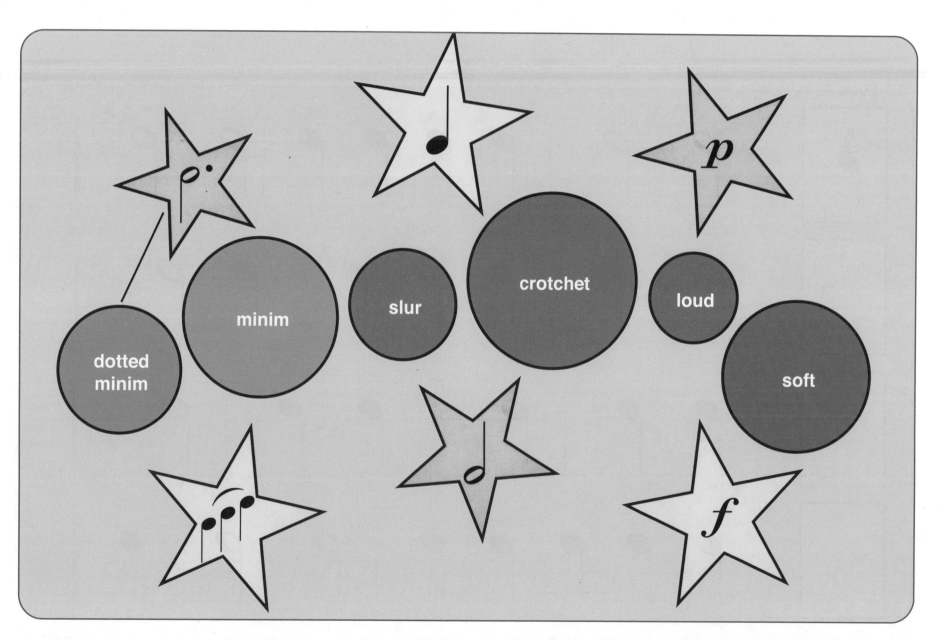

Colour the circles:

Red for repeated notes   Green for thirds

Yellow for seconds   Blue for fourths

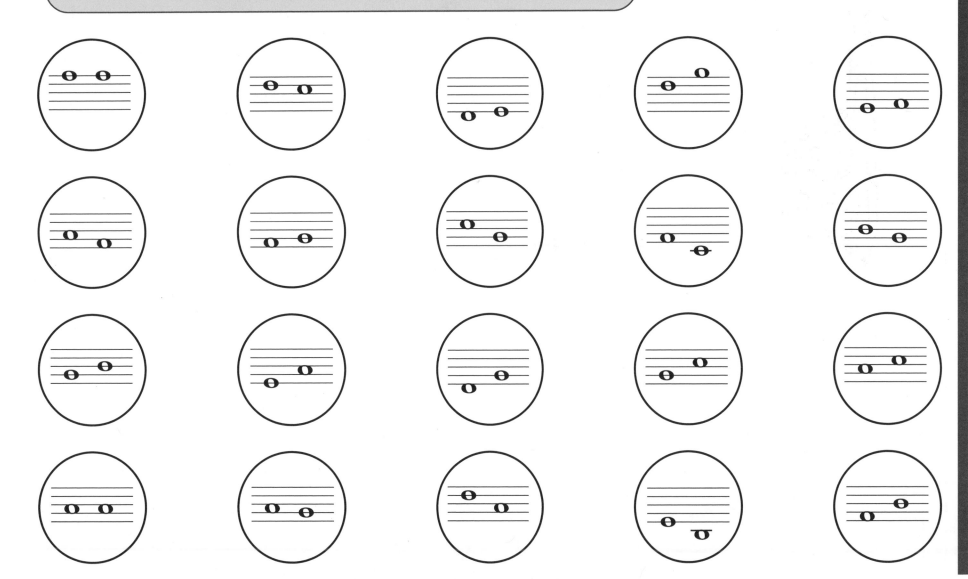

Write the letters of the music alphabet
in these notes going up.

Write the letters of the music alphabet
in these notes going down.

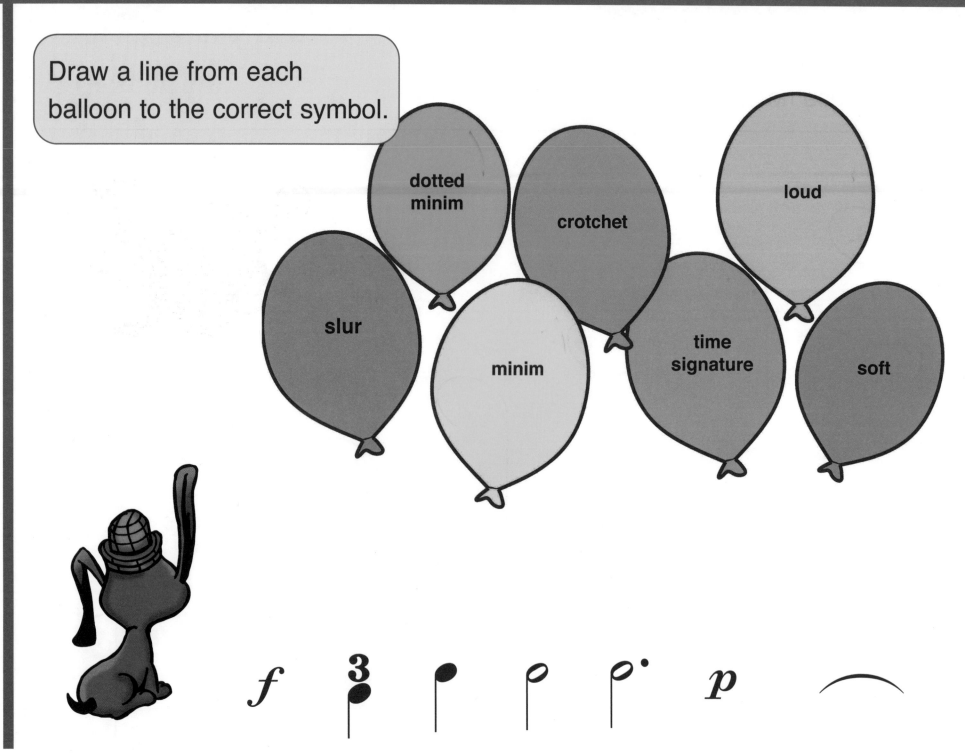

Draw a line from each balloon to the correct symbol.

Draw an **X** through the one interval
in each group of boxes that is different.

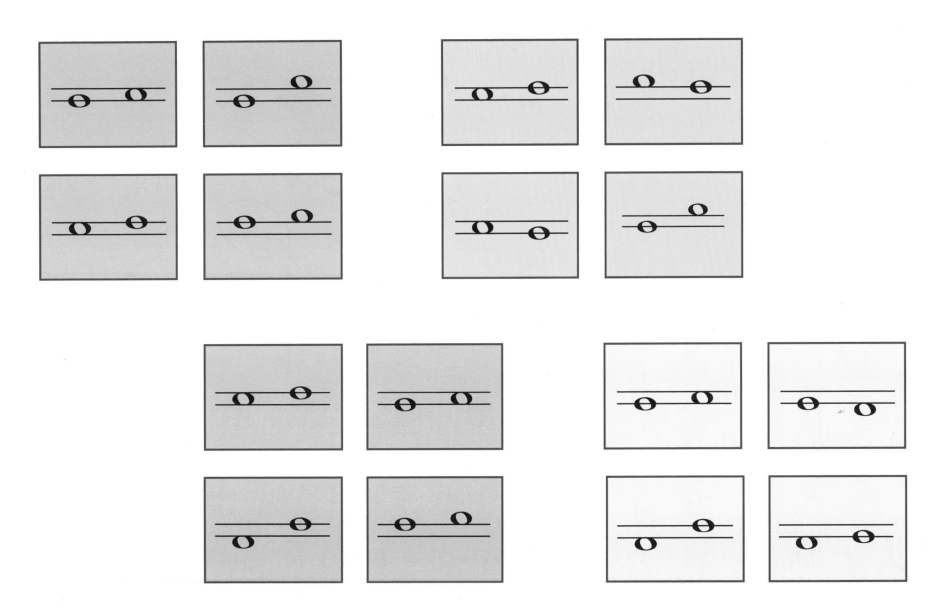

Write the letter names of the notes
going up, down, or repeating.

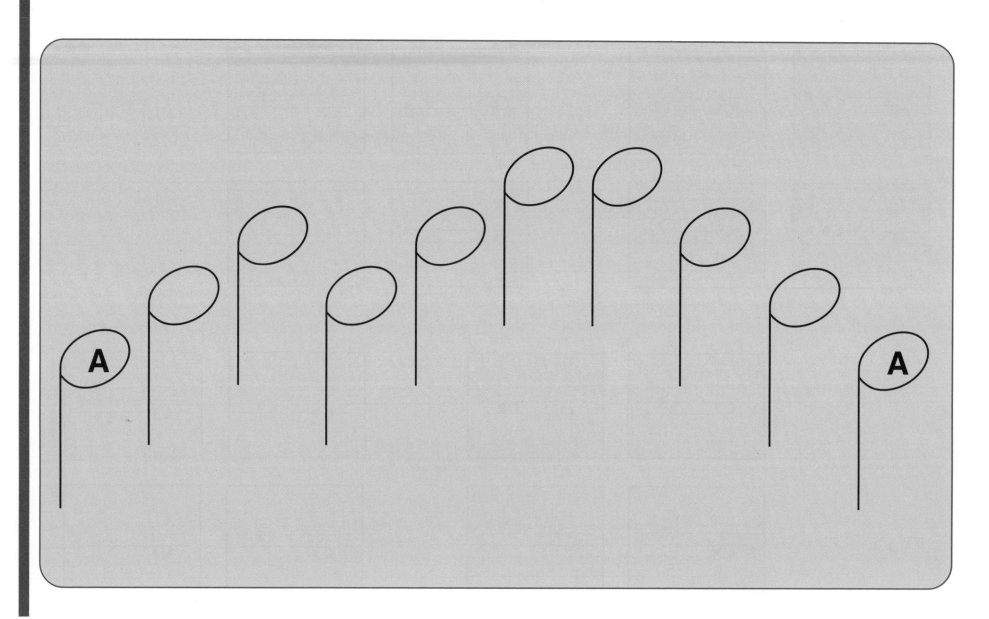

Write the letter names of the notes going up, down, or repeating.

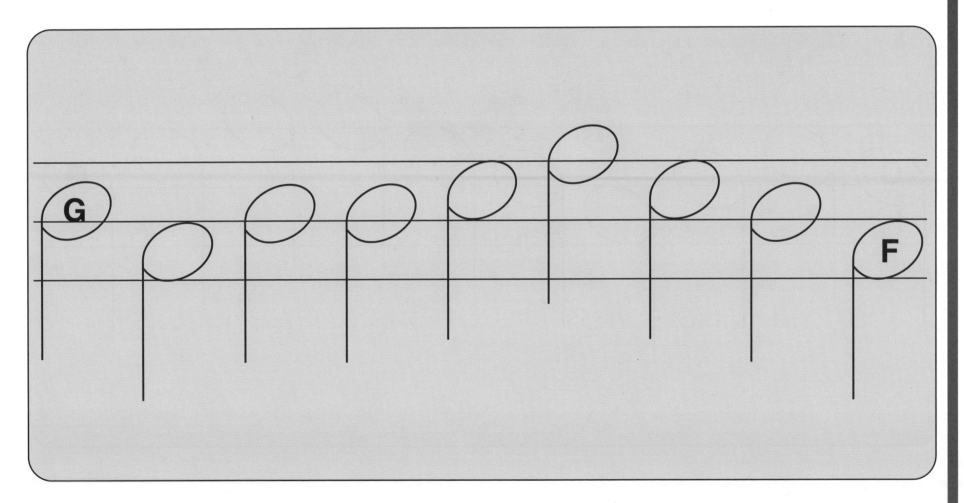

Write the names of the notes going up, down, or repeating.

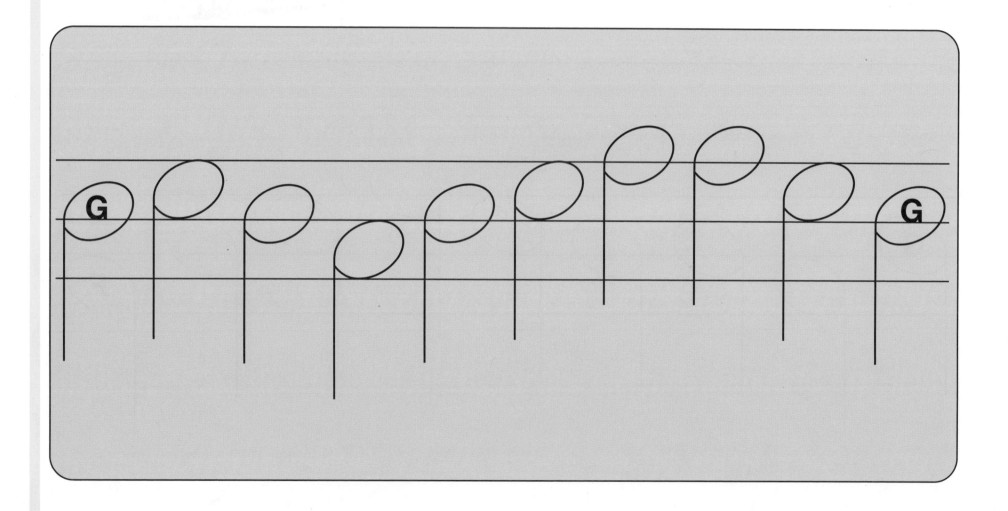

Music Math

Add or subtract the notes in each problem.
The first one is done to show you how.

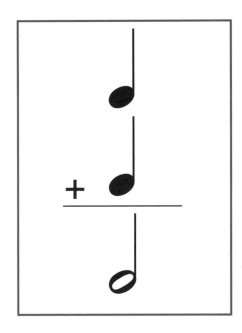

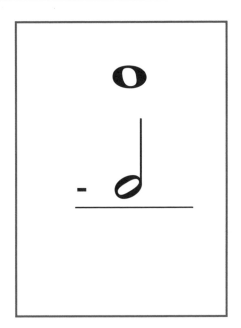

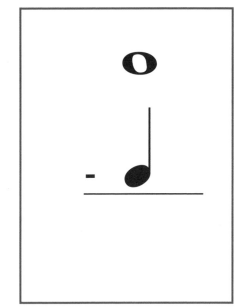

Follow all the fifths to help Bobo find Chip.

Bobo

Chip

Write the names of the notes going up, down, or repeating.

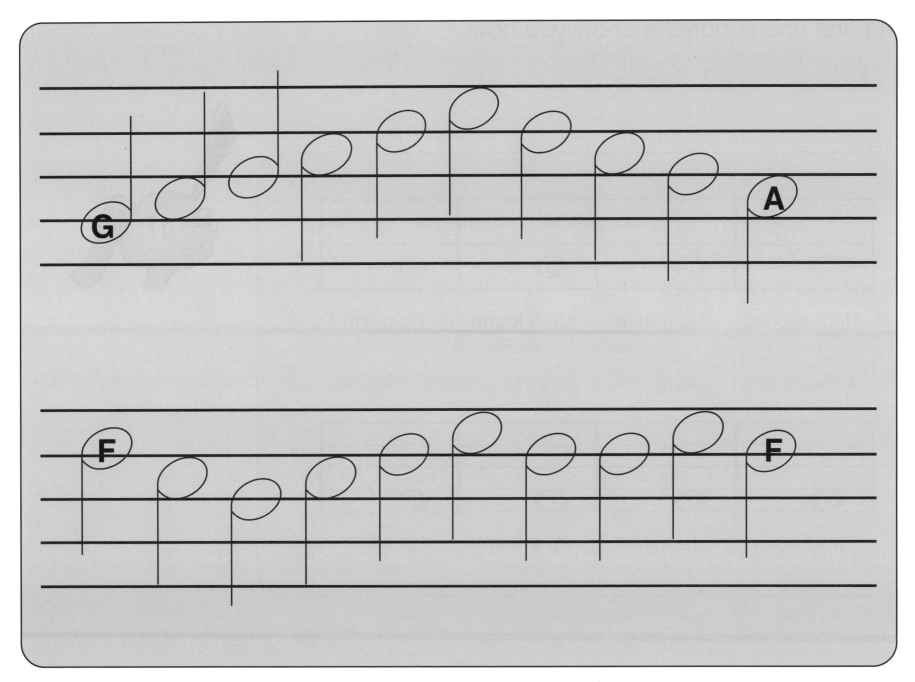

In each bar, draw the second note and write its letter name.

The first one is done to show you how.

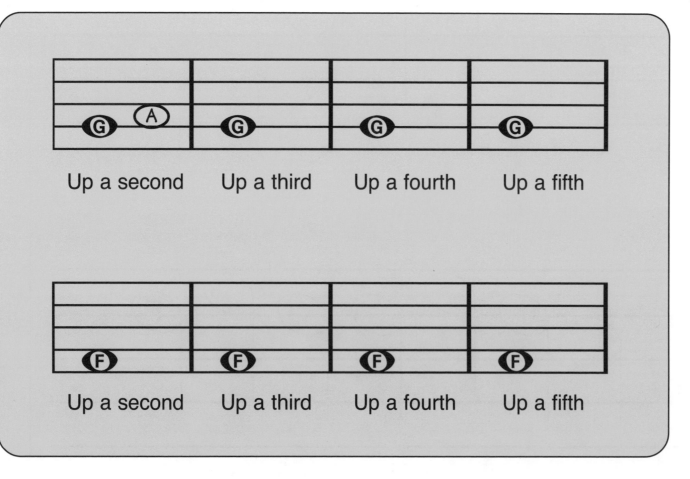

Rhythm Detective

Find and circle the bars that have too many beats.
The first one is done to show you how.

Write the music alphabet going up by thirds.

To help you, the letters in between are shown in gray.

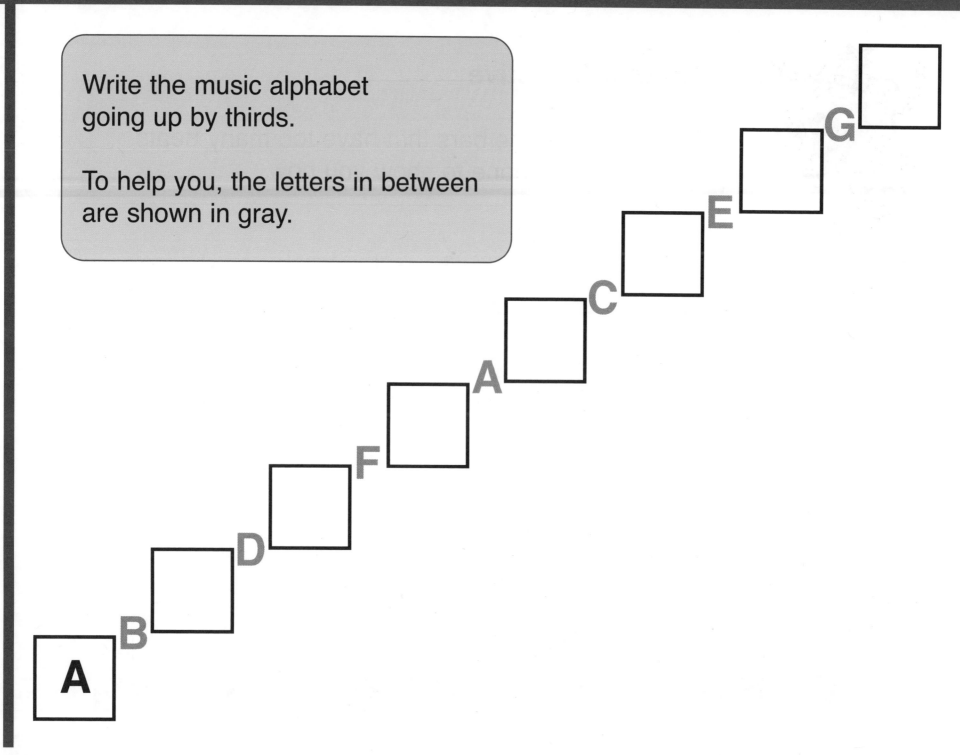

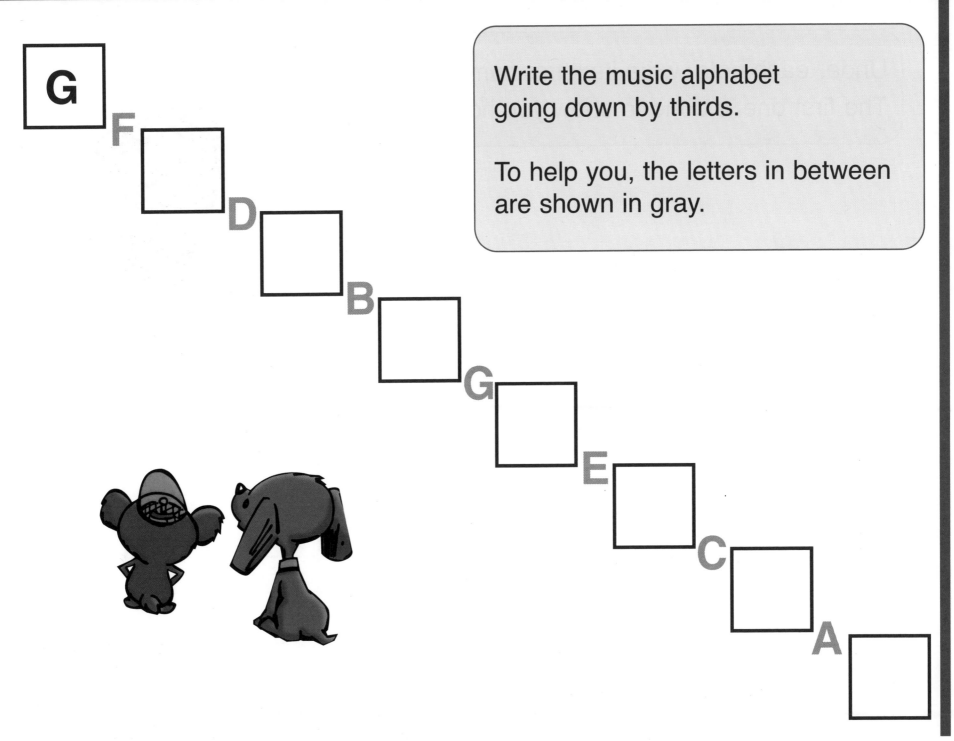

G

F

D

B

G

E

C

A

Write the music alphabet going down by thirds.

To help you, the letters in between are shown in gray.

Under each note, write its letter name.
The first one is done to show you how.

A Musical Rainbow

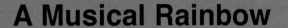

Colour the Bass F red.
Colour the bass clef violet.
Colour the semibreve green.

Colour the Middle C yellow.
Colour the Treble G orange.
Colour the treble clef blue.

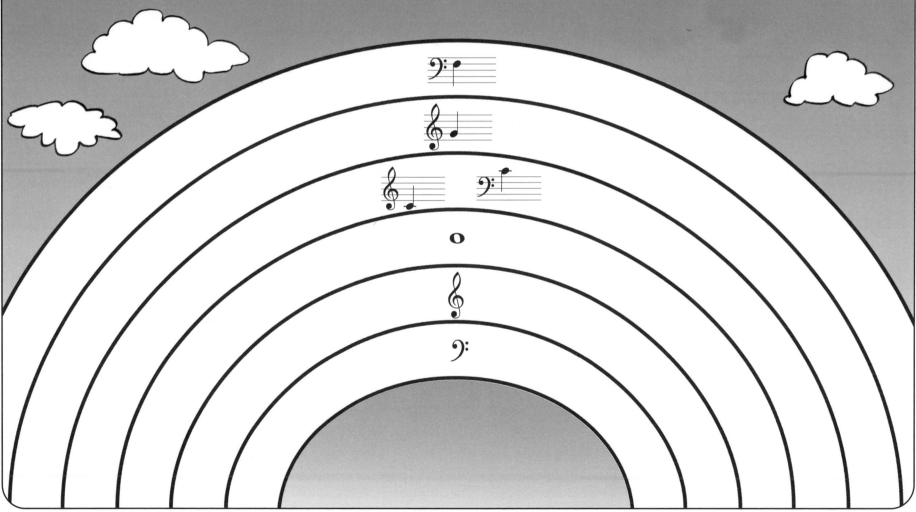

GLOSSARY

READING

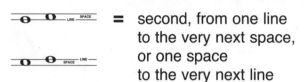 = second, from one line to the very next space, or one space to the very next line

= third, from one line to the next line, or one space to the next space

= fourth, line to space, skipping one line; or space to line, skipping one line

= fifth, space to space, skipping a space; or line to line, skipping a line

𝄢 = F clef

= Bass stave

𝄞 = G clef

= Treble stave

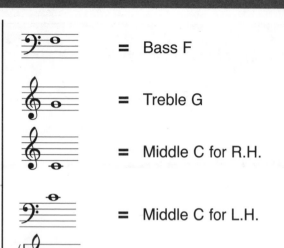

= Bass F

= Treble G

= Middle C for R.H.

= Middle C for L.H.

= Grand staff

RHYTHM

 = crotchet

= minim, as long as two crotchets

= dotted minim, as long as three crotchets

= semibreve, as long as four crotchets

4/4 = time signature

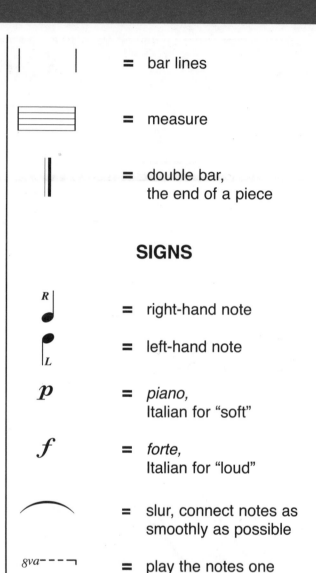

= bar lines

= measure

= double bar, the end of a piece

SIGNS

= right-hand note

= left-hand note

p = *piano,* Italian for "soft"

f = *forte,* Italian for "loud"

= slur, connect notes as smoothly as possible

8va = play the notes one octave higher

8va = play the notes one octave lower